SEO FOR BEGINNERS

SIMPLE SEO STRATEGIES TO 10X
WEB TRAFFIC OVERNIGHT AND
INSTANTLY OPTIMIZE VISIBILITY
ON TOP SEARCH ENGINES
GOOGLE, BING AND YAHOO

© Copyright 2017 by Tony Robson
All rights reserved.

This document is geared towards providing exact and reliable information regarding the topic and issue covered. The publication is sold with the idea that the publisher is not required to render accounting, officially permitted, or otherwise, qualified services. If advice is necessary, legal or professional, a practiced individual in the profession should be ordered.

- From a Declaration of Principles which was accepted and approved equally by a Committee of the American Bar Association and a Committee of Publishers and Associations.

In no way is it legal to reproduce, duplicate, or transmit any part of this document in either electronic means or in printed format. Recording of this publication is strictly prohibited and any storage of this document is not allowed unless with written permission from the publisher. All rights reserved.

The information provided herein is stated to be truthful and consistent, in that any liability, in terms of inattention or otherwise, by any usage or abuse of any policies, processes, or directions contained within is the solitary and utter responsibility of the recipient reader. Under no circumstances will any legal responsibility or blame be held against the publisher for any reparation, damages, or monetary loss due to the information herein, either directly or indirectly.

Respective authors own all copyrights not held by the publisher.

The information herein is offered for informational purposes solely, and is universal as so. The presentation of the information is without contract or any type of guarantee assurance.

The trademarks that are used are without any consent, and the publication of the trademark is without permission or backing by the trademark owner. All trademarks and brands within this book are for clarifying purposes only and are the owned by the owners themselves, not affiliated with this document.

Table of Contents

Introduction 1

<u>CHAPTER 1</u>
Understanding SEO 3

<u>CHAPTER 2</u>
SEO Operation.. 13

<u>CHAPTER 3</u>
SEO Techniques & Strategies 23

<u>CHAPTER 4</u>
SEO Services and Usability 33

<u>CHAPTER 5</u>
5 SEO Hacks You Can Do Right Now to Rank Your Website Higher 41

Conclusion 49

Preview Of Snapchat Marketing For Business......... 51

Introduction

Thank you for downloading "*SEO for Beginners: Simple SEO Strategies to 10x Web Traffic Overnight and Instantly Optimize Visibility on Top Search Engines Google, Bing and Yahoo*".

This book contains powerful steps and strategies on driving traffic to your website, as well as increase visibility on Google, Bing, and Yahoo. The result will be that you are able to rank higher on these search engines, and thus able to generate much more traffic. The magic of this book occurs in the ability to be able to understand the nuances of SEO, which will allow you to be a step ahead of your competition. The goal of this e-book is for you to be well-versed in SEO, as well as the ability to do this on your own using these strategies.

With proven studies and examples, this book will help you in understanding the different aspects, types and implementations/operations of SEO. As it is through only complete understanding and absorption of the utmost knowledge of a concept that you can master it, this book shall provide you with a detailed account into the different aspects and perspectives of this subsequent internet marketing tool. Hence providing with subsequent strategies and procedures that are suitable for the users requirement.

Thanks again for downloading this book, I hope you enjoy it!

CHAPTER 1

Understanding SEO

Marketing, as most people know it, is a form of reaching buyers for a product or service. Currently, a business simply can't survive without having at least a basic marketing plan. It's how any business attracts buyers, and the biggest players in the field use marketing to their advantage. Amazon is my favorite example of a company who is taking marketing to a new level. They simply are outperforming their competition in all aspects, including utilizing SEO, Facebook, and other social media platforms to lure you back to their addictive website. SEO is one piece of the puzzle that can make your website stand out from your competition when they are searching for your product or service on the top search engines. Let's now get into what exactly Search Engine Optimization is, and how the processes work.

As the field of marketing continues to expand, some aspects have become essential for businesses to thrive in this ever-growing marketplace. Marketing of a business mainly aims on a business demographic awareness and popularity, but these principles would be useless without ease in accessibility of said product or service. This however is an overlying problem in the diverse and crowded marketplace that is the internet. Hence, to standout and to find specific services and products, SEO is an integral tool that is used to fulfill this purpose.

Search Engine Optimization, or SEO as most call it, is the process of maximizing the number of visitors to a website by ensuring that the site appears high on the list of results returned by a search engine. In many respects, it's simply quality control for websites. From a different angle, SEO can be described as a marketing discipline focused on growing visibility in organic (non-paid) search engine results. SEO encompasses both the technical and creative elements required to improve rankings, drive traffic, and increase awareness in search engines. There are many aspects to SEO, from the words on your page to the way other sites link to you on the web. Oftentimes, SEO is simply a matter of making sure your site is structured in a way that search engines understand. SEO isn't just about building search engine-friendly websites. It's about making your site better for people too.

In the present day, the majority of web traffic is driven by the major commercial search engines, Google, Bing, and Yahoo. Although social media and other types of traffic can generate visits to your website, search engines are the primary method of navigation for most Internet users. This is true whether your site provides content, services, products, information, or just about anything else. Search engines are unique in that they provide targeted traffic—people looking for what you offer. Search engines are the roadways that make this happen. If search engines cannot find your site, or add your content to their databases, you miss out on incredible opportunities to drive traffic to your site.

Search queries—the words that users type into the search box—carry extraordinary value. Simply put, search engine traffic can make (or break) an organization's success. Targeted traffic to a website can provide publicity, revenue, and exposure like no other channel of marketing. Investing time and energy into an SEO campaign can have an exceptional ROI (Return on Investment) compared to other types of marketing and promotion. Search engines are smart, but they still need help to rank the deserving sites for targeted keywords. The major search engines are always working to improve their technology to crawl through the web more deeply and return better results to users. However, there is a limit to how efficiently search engines can operate. Where the correct execution of SEO can net a website thousands of visitors and increased attention, the wrong moves can hide or bury your site deep in the search results where visibility is minimal. In addition to making content available to search engines, SEO also helps boost rankings so that content will be placed where searchers will readily find it. The Internet is becoming increasingly competitive, and those companies who correctly implement these principles will have an unfair advantage in attracting visitors and customers.

As we've already noted, it's tough getting noticed on the Web. A Web page can provide useful information about a popular subject in an interactive and engrossing way, yet still attract few visitors. One of the most reliable ways to improve traffic is to achieve a high ranking on search engine return pages (SERPs). Assume that you've created the definitive Web site on a subject -- we'll use skydiving as an example. Your site is so new that it's not even listed on any SERPs yet, so your first step is to submit your site to search engines like Google and Yahoo.

The Web pages on your skydiving site include useful information, exciting photographs and helpful links guiding visitors to other resources. Even with the best information about skydiving on the Web, your site may not crack the top page of results on major search engines. When people search for the term "skydiving," they could end up going to inferior Web sites because yours isn't in the top results.

While most search engine companies try to keep their processes a secret, their criteria for high spots on SERPs isn't a complete mystery. Search engines are successful only if they provide a user links to the best Web sites related to the user's search terms. If your site is the best skydiving resource on the Web, it benefits search engines to list the site high up on their SERPs. You just have to find a way to show search engines that your site belongs at the top of the heap. That's where SEO comes in -- it's a collection of techniques a webmaster can use to improve his or her site's SERP position.

Building a strong website and providing clear navigation will help search engines index your site quickly and easily. This will also, more importantly, provide visitors with a good experience of using your site and encourage repeat visits. It's worth considering that Google is increasingly paying attention to user experience. When it comes to how much traffic is driven by search engines to your website, the percentage is substantial, and perhaps the clearest indicator of the importance of SEO. In 2014, Conductor suggested 64% of all web traffic comes from organic search, compared to 2% from social, 6% from paid search, 12% direct and 15% from other referral sources. This tallies with our own data, with approximately 70-75% of SEW traffic coming from organic. Of all organic traffic, in 2015 it was found that Google accounts for more than 90% of global organic search traffic. So obviously you need a strong presence on Google SERPs, but how strong? Well, according to a study from Advanced Web Ranking (which I've trotted out before when discussing how to dominate Google) shows that on the first SERP, the top five results accounts for 67.60% of all clicks and the results from six to 10 accounts for only 3.73%.

Although Google is continuously refining how they rank web pages, there remain two key elements that are the foundation for successful results:

Onsite – your content and website infrastructure

- targeting the best keyword clusters

- matching existing content to target specific keyword clusters
- creating new content to target specific keyword clusters
- having the best website infrastructure and architecture

Offsite – how your website is referred to from other online sources

- developing a profile of high quality, on-theme incoming links
- having a relevant and active social media presence
- creating citations (non-linking references) about you
- at least half of your SEO outcomes are influenced by elements outside your direct control

Types of SEO

As the colors of the types of SEO suggest, there are stark differences in the approach and long-term results of white hat and black hat SEO. Though both types of SEO have their proponents, most companies/websites with long-term, stable, and sustainable goals will tend to stay away from the dark-colored variety.

	White Hat SEO	Black Hat SEO
Definition	White hat SEO utilizes techniques and methods to improve the search engine rankings of a website which don't run afoul of search engine (mainly Google) guidelines.	Black Hat SEO exploits weaknesses in the search engine algorithms to obtain high rankings for a website. Such techniques and methods are in direct conflict with search engine guidelines.
Wholesomeness Level	High	Very Low (not wholesome at all if you ask those in charge of cleaning search engine result page spam)

	White Hat SEO	**Black Hat SEO**
Techniques	Some white hat SEO techniques include: high quality content development, website HTML optimization and restructuring, link acquisition campaigns supported by high quality content and manual research and outreach.	Some black hat SEO techniques include: link spam, keyword stuffing, cloaking, hidden text, and hidden links.
What to Expect	Steady, gradual, but lasting growth in rankings.	Quick, unpredictable, and short-lasting growth in rankings.

The work of most SEO companies, however, operates in a gray area, aptly named Gray Hat SEO. Whether by design or pressure from clients to deliver results, many SEO companies try to deliver solutions and results for customers by utilizing techniques which don't quite cross the line into black hat SEO, but are well outside of what would be considered white hat SEO. Gray hat SEO is recognizable by 'affordable' pricing, since the SEO company must reduce cost by resorting to questionable techniques to deliver results, instead of highly involved campaign activities.

In the end, this book highlights that there is no 'right' or 'wrong' ways to do SEO, but those shopping for SEO services should be aware of the different types and approaches so that they know the level of risk they are taking on.

CHAPTER 2

SEO Operation

What are search engines looking for?

When it comes time to optimize SEO for a website, a user must know the virtues of the operation an SEO tool may possess. Hence, it is important for beginners looking to integrate SEO to be equipped with knowledge behind each operating skill:

1) Relevancy

Search engines try to provide the most relevant results to a searcher's query, whether it's a simple answer to the question "how old is Ryan Gosling?" to more complicated queries such as "what is the best steak restaurant near me?" How search engines provide these results is down to their own internal algorithms, which we'll probably never truly determine, but there are factors that you can be certain will influence these results and they're all based around relevancy... For instance: a searcher's location, their search history, time of day/year, etc.

2) Quality of Content

Do you regularly publish helpful, useful articles, videos or other types of media that are popular and well produced? Do you write for actual human beings rather than the search engine itself? Latest research from Searchmetrics on ranking factors indicates that Google is moving further towards longer-form content that understands a visitor's intention, instead of using keywords based on popular search queries to create content.

It's amazing how simply focusing on the user experience will improve the rankings of a website. You can't put lipstick on a pig, as they say (no offense, pigs).

3) User experience

There are many SEO benefits for providing the best possible user experience. An easily navigable, clearly searchable site with relevant internal linking and related content. The goal is to keep visitors on your webpage and hungry to explore further.

4) Site speed

How quickly a website loads is increasingly becoming

a differentiator for search engines. Google may soon start labeling results that are hosted on Accelerated Mobile Page (AMP) so this could potentially be an issue for many websites moving forward.

5) Cross-device compatibility

Is your website optimized for any given screen size or device? Bear in mind that Google has stated that responsive design is its preferred method of mobile optimization.

6) Internal linking

We've talked about the benefits of ensuring your site has clear and easy-to-use navigation, but there's also a practice that editors and writers can carry out when publishing articles to help push traffic around the site and that may lead to higher trust signals for Google: internal linking. (See what we did there.)

Internal linking has many advantages:

It provides your audience with further reading options. As long as they're relevant and you use clear anchor text (the clickable highlighted words in any give link). This can help reduce your bounce rates.

It helps to improve your ranking for certain keywords. If we want this article to rank for the term 'SEO basics' then we can begin linking to it from other posts using variations of similar anchor text. This tells Google that this post is relevant to people searching for 'SEO basics'. Some experts recommend varying your anchor text pointing to the same page as Google may see multiple identical uses as 'suspicious'.

It helps Google crawl and index your site. Those little Googlebots that are sent out to fetch new information on your site will have a better idea of how useful and trustworthy your content is, the more they crawl through your internal links.

7) Authority

An authority website is a site that is trusted by its users, the industry it operates in, as well as other websites and search engines. Traditionally, a link from an authority website is very valuable, as it's seen as a vote of confidence. The more of these you have, and the higher quality content you produce, the more likely your own site will become an authority too. However, as the Search metric research suggests, year-on-year correlations between backlinks and rankings are decreasing, so perhaps over time 'links' may not be as important to SEO as we once thought. There's a good argument raging in the comments to this recent piece on links as a marketing KPI, which offers some diverse views on the subject.

8) Meta descriptions and Title Tags

Having a meta description won't necessarily improve your ranking on the SERP, but it is something that should be used before publishing an article as it can help increase your chances of a searcher clicking on your result. The meta description is the short paragraph of text that appears under your page's URL in the search results, it's also something you should have complete control of in your CMS.

Write succinctly (under 156 characters is good), clearly, and make sure it's relevant to your headline and the content of the article itself. Title tags are used to tell search engines and visitors what your site is about in the most concise and accurate way possible. The keywords in your title tag show up highlighted in search engine results (if the query uses those keywords), as well as in your browser tab and when sharing your site externally.

You can write your own title tag inside the <head> area of your site's HTML:

<head>
<title>

Example

Title</title>
</head>

You should use a few accurate keywords describing the page as well as your own brand name. Only use relevant keywords though, and the most important thing to consider is that although you are formatting for search engines, you should write for humans.

9) Schema markup

You can make your search results appear more attractive by adding Schema markup to the HTML of your pages. This can help turn your search results into a rich media playground, adding star-ratings, customer ratings, images, and various other bits of helpful info. Schema is also the preferred method of markup by most search engines including Google, and it's straightforward to use.

10) Properly tagged images

Many people forget to include the alt attribute when they upload images to their content, but this is something you shouldn't overlook because Google cannot 'see' your images, but can 'read' the alt text. By describing your image in the alt text as accurately as possible it will increase the chances of your images appearing in Google Image search. It will also improve the accessibility of your site for people using 'screen reader' software.

11) Keyword Research

Every day, 25% of the search terms inputted into the top engines have never been searched before. So, we focus on creating what we call "keyword clusters" – groups of keyword phrases focused around high volume "core" keyword phrases. For example, a core keyword phrase might be "accommodation" and that cluster may include "accommodation New York", "luxury accommodation" and "boutique accommodation". Using the latest SEO tools and software, it is our job to find you the optimum balance in your keyword phrase list to be targeted, that delivers the best ROI (Return on Investment).

12) Matching – Existing and New Content

Our approach to Onsite SEO is to try to match one keyword phrase from each keyword cluster to a single page on your website. Typically, a home page will be focused on a "gun" keyword phrase, while a main navigation page will target the next most important keyword phrases. Often, a website won't have web pages to target some of the important keyword phrases you will want to target; in this case we work with you to create new pages to reach these terms.

13) Behind the Scenes – The Code

Not all websites are created equal. Some websites are great and are ideally search engine-friendly, but many we come across are not. A key part of our role is to assist you and your web developer to ensure that as many pages of your website are correctly indexed and that there are no technical impediments to your online success. Yes, "look and feel" is vitally important in motivating visitors to explore your website, and in guiding them to act or buy…but they need to find your website first.

14) Offsite Link Profile

In the simplest of terms, a Search Engine sees a link from another website to your website as being like a vote of confidence in your web site. Search Engines believe that if other websites are linking to your web pages, you must have something good to link to and a Search Engine will rate your page that is being linked to more positively. Today Search Engines take into consideration many additional factors other than just the sheer number of links when evaluating your offsite link profile:

- the Reputation or Trust value of sites linking to your web site
- the Theme or Relevance of sites linking to you
- the "Anchor Text" (the words that the link is embedded behind) in links to your site

15) Offsite Social Profile

More and more, the Search Engines are starting to consider social media references as important signals about your website and your company in general. It's not just about having a Facebook page, a Twitter account or a Google Plus page, but also how active you are and in what manner your social media associates refer to you, your company and your website content.

16) Offsite Citation Profile

Citations are references to you company name, address, phone number or website that may not actually link to you but are recognizable to Search Engines. Although these citations are indeed helpful across the board, they are particularly useful in enhancing your Search Results in the Search Engines' maps and geo-location rankings.

CHAPTER 3

SEO Techniques & Strategies

As we've discussed in depth, SEO is a way to attain high rankings in organic search engine results. SEO should never be the sole means of marketing any business, because search engine algorithms are in constant flux, and any one of (on average) daily changes can impact a website's ranking negatively, to a point where the entire business can be put in jeopardy. So, organic rankings should never be the sole source of traffic for any website that is being run as a business. With that said, SEO can contribute greatly to almost any online marketing campaign.

SEO is a long-term process, especially if it is to contribute in a tangible fashion to the bottom line of an online marketing effort. It is a mid- to long-term solution which does require time to produce results. So, if you have just started an online business (or one that has an online component) and are looking a way to jumpstart your website traffic, SEO is not for you.

There is often a misunderstanding in what an SEO campaign can realistically accomplish. As stated multiple times, SEO is not magic, nor is it an exact science where an action will have a specific and completely predictable reaction. No SEO company can produce high rankings for its clients by simply offering directory submissions, and half-witted articles written by college dropouts who hire out their writing skill so unscrupulous SEO companies for pennies per word.

While most search engine companies try to keep their processes a secret, their criteria for high spots on SERPs isn't a complete mystery. Search engines are successful only if they provide a user links to the best Web sites related to the user's search terms. You must find a way to show search engines that your site belongs at the top of the heap. That's where SEO comes in -- it's a collection of techniques a webmaster can use to improve his or her site's SERP position.

Experts in SEO can tell you the steps you need to take to be one of the top entries on a SERP. In an ideal World Wide Web, your site would rise to the top of every search engine's skydiving SERP based on content alone. While it's possible for your site to take the No. 1 SERP spot on its own, it could take months or even longer. Even worse, there's no guarantee your skydiving site will ever make it as high as the first page of search results. For some webmasters, site traffic isn't that big a deal -- their sites might be a personal project. But for anyone who uses the Web to make money, it's crucial. Whether the webmaster makes money by selling products on the site or through hosting Web advertisements, more visitors translates into more money. That's why some large companies are willing to spend money on SEO consultants -- they can be a worthy investment if the company's site is ranked higher than competitor sites.

SEO techniques rely on how search engines work. Some are legitimate methods that are a great way to let search engines know your Web page exists. Other techniques aren't good ways to get noticed and might involve exploiting a search engine so that it gives the page a higher ranking. Sometimes it's tough to tell if an approach is legitimate. If it seems a little questionable, it's probably a bad idea.

To fully understand and successfully adapt SEO in the business' marketing framework, the company should adapt the following strategies in order to obtain the best results:

1. Optimize for mobile search and browsing

Mobile optimization has been important for years. However, in October 2016 mobile overtook desktop with mobile and tablet accounting for 51.3 percent of all web browsing. Around this same time (November 2016), Google launched their mobile-first index. Previously, Google crawled the desktop version of a site, using that as their primary search engine index. However, with this update, Google has now started to use the mobile version of a site as its primary index. This means prioritizing your mobile site and mobile content is a must.

2. Engage in intentional link building

Links have been the most important driver of rankings for years now. Google has confirmed they're one of the top three ranking factors (along with content and RankBrain), and multiple ranking factor studies have confirmed this. A recent study from Stone Temple seems to indicate that links are even more powerful than we thought. However, they also found that links alone aren't enough to redeem low-quality content. Their advice, "If your content is not relevant or competitive, links won't help your ranking. If it is, links will make the difference."

3. Optimize for voice search

According to KPCB's 2016 Internet Trends Report, voice search queries have seen more than a 35X increase since 2008 and more than a 7x increase since 2010. The report also cites Andrew Ng, Chief Scientist at Baidu, as saying, "As speech recognition accuracy goes from say 95% to 99%, all of us in the room will go from barely using it today to using it all the time. Most people underestimate the difference between 95% and 99% accuracy - 99% is a game changer..." It's only a matter of time before we hit that 99% mark. Prepare now by optimizing your content for voice search.

4. Optimize for Rich Answers

As of 2015, Rich Answers were displayed for nearly 20% of all queries. This number is likely to be significantly higher in 2017. If you want your content to show for common industry-related questions, it's vital that you intentionally optimize for these queries. There are many ways you can do this, including explicitly asking the question in your content, including a direct answer followed by more in-depth backup info, using lists and creating Q&A pages.

5. Consider using shorter URLs

Using descriptive, keyword-relevant URLs has been an effective SEO strategy for years. However, some research seems to indicate that using shorter URLs may lead to higher rankings. While there's no set number of words you should include, Google has indicated in the past that anything after the first five words won't be given as much credit. Whenever possible, use your primary keywords in the first few words of your URL, and try to keep your entire URL to around five words total.

6. Local optimization is a must

Given the move toward a mobile-first mindset, it's no surprise that many experts are placing increased emphasis on local search these days. If you have a local component to your business, optimizing for local search in 2017 is imperative. As more of your customers turn to mobile to find local businesses, products and information, getting found for local keywords is a must.

7. Focus on improving user experience

We've known for years that providing a good user

experience is the key to rankings. However, the connection between user experience metrics (click-through rates, bounce rates, etc.) has always been a indirect one. There is a direct connection between high rankings and beating out the expected CTR of other pages in the SERPs. In other words, if your content shows up in the SERPs but doesn't outperform the other results in terms of clicks, you may not hold onto your rankings for long. One of the most important things you can do to ensure your CTRs remain strong is to optimize your metadata for your chosen keywords. Remember: Your title tag and meta description act as your ad copy in the SERPs, and should engage viewers and entice them to click-through.

8. Use related keywords in your content

Keyword research is still a critically-important aspect of SEO. However, it shouldn't just be about finding one or two words or phrases to use in your content. Ideally, look for phrases that are semantically-connected to your main topic. For instance, if I'm writing a blog post about making a black forest cake, I'll most likely need to use words like "cherries", "chocolate" and "whipped cream." Using these words will prove to Google that I'm comprehensively covering my topic.

It will also mean I have a much more balanced and detailed article -- which is great for user experience.

9. Write longer content

It's not only content length that leads to increased rankings but content quality: The goal isn't to simply write 2,000 words of rambling content. No, size matters, but so does the quality in that size. It needs to be well written for starters, and it can't go off on tangents. The content must be laser-focused. Anecdotal evidence aside, virtually every study done to date shows a correlation between longer content and higher rankings. Some suggest 1,200-1,300 words, while others say 1500 words should be the minimum. If you want your content to rank, I suggest aiming for a minimum length of 1,200 words for standard blog posts, and 2,000 words+ for evergreen content.

10. Speed up your site

For years, Google has been emphasizing the need to have a fast site. However, considering the upcoming mobile-first index, I imagine site speed will become an even more significant ranking factor in 2017. In September, Google again emphasized the importance of speed, particularly in relation to mobile devices: "Slow loading sites frustrate users and negatively impact publishers. In our new study, "The Need for Mobile Speed," we found that 53 percent of mobile site visits are abandoned if pages take longer than 3 seconds to load."

11. Aim for high topical authority

If you're writing long-form, comprehensive content there's a good chance you're already achieving this. However, it's too important a strategy not to explicitly spell out. In a recent analysis of 1 million search results, Brian Dean of Backlinko found that comprehensive content vastly outranked more shallow content. He even found that pages that comprehensively covered a topic outranked shorter content that was highly-optimized for a certain keyword - even when the comprehensive page didn't use that keyword at all.

In other words, focus more on the depth and breadth of your content rather than on word count and keywords. This will undoubtedly be better for rankings as well as user experience.

12. Focus on user intent

Since the one-to-one relationship between keywords and rankings is now gone -- or is at least significantly diminished -- optimizing for intent is even more crucial. This will mean focusing not just on specific keywords, but on the meaning and motivation behind those words and phrases. What are people looking for when they use those queries? What long tail phrases should I be using to attract highly-relevant visitors? Which keywords should I focus on to drive conversions and not just traffic?

CHAPTER 4

SEO Services and Usability

Website SEO Audit

An SEO audit can come in varying levels of detail and complexity. A simple website audit can be as short as a few pages long, and would address glaring on-page issues such as missing titles, and lack of content. On the other end of the spectrum, a comprehensive website SEO audit will be comprised of dozens of pages (for most larger sites it will be over one hundred pages) and address even the tiniest of website elements which may potentially be detrimental to the ranking-ability of a website. With a basic audit, a website owner should expect to receive a well thought out guide for not only fixing elements of the website which are not search engine friendly, but also guidance for going beyond addressing issues, and making marked improvements in areas of content, link development, and overall organic search strategy. It is important to realize that even though having a search engine friendly website is the first crucial step towards attaining improved rankings, there is no guarantee that the implementation of recommendations from an SEO audit will catapult a website's rankings to the top of search engine result pages (SERPs). SEO results take time, and require diligent maintenance in order to produce reliable and stable rankings.

On-Page SEO

On-page (sometimes called on-site) SEO is the process of implementing the necessary changes as recommended by an SEO audit. These changes can be implemented by the website owner (if they have the capability) or an SEO company. On-page SEO should be part of all SEO packages, as it is the foundation up on which a successful SEO campaign must be built. On-page SEO addresses a variety of fundamental elements (as they relate to SEO) such as page titles, headings, content and content organization, and internal link structure. As with a website SEO audit, there are basic, as well as comprehensive services when it comes to on-page SEO. At the most basic level, an on-page optimization campaign can be a one-time project which includes recommendations developed through an audit, and the implementation thereof. This type of on-page optimization would generally target the home page and a few other important pages on the website. More comprehensive on-page SEO campaigns will use the findings of a highly-detailed website SEO audit, and monitor results to guide ongoing changes to the on-page optimization. Even though on-page work does not need to be updated in many cases (e.g. when the site has evergreen content), it is recommended that the website and the content being published therein be audited on a regular basis to uncover potential problems which may creep up through website updates and changes.

SEO Content Development

SEO content development is the process of creating website content which can come in a variety of forms, including text e.g. articles, whitepapers, essays, research documents, tutorials, and glossaries, infographics (information graphics), PDFs, searchable databases, web tools, and the like. As you will note, the traditional definition of content is no longer appropriate, since content comes in many forms. It is also important to realize that depending on your niche, not every type of content would be suitable for your website.

'SEO content' is also a misnomer; content which can impact search engine friendliness positively should be more accurately described as "high quality content", which will in turn make earning and acquiring links much easier. When looking for content that is going to help your SEO efforts, it is crucial to look for high quality content; or more accurately, find people who can develop such content. Seeking out 'SEO content' can lead to content that is jammed full of keywords without much consideration for quality.SEO content writing as a service can be useful, if shortcuts are not taken, and the content is not expected to perform magic. Well written, interesting and useful content will inevitably be found, and get attention on its own merits; however, it also helps lay the foundation for a successful link development campaign.

Link Development

Link development is one of the most controversial and often talked (written) about topics of the SEO industry. Since backlinks are the most vital component of any SEO campaign, and at the same time the most time consuming and consequently most expensive (assuming they are good quality links and not just random directory submissions and blog comment spam) part, inevitably, there are many service providers who offer inexpensive link building services to attract and impress potential clients. Such schemes include large volumes of directory submissions (e.g., 200 directory submissions per month), worthless blog and forum comment spam (e.g., 100 blog links per month), or article writing and submissions which result in extremely poor quality content published on equally low-quality article directories which contribute in no positive way to ranking improvements. So if someone is quoting you a $500 per month SEO services which includes large volumes of directory submissions, blog posts, articles, blog/forum comments and so on, all you will be doing is throwing your money away. This is not to say that you can't get link-work for $500 per month; however, it won't be for a large volume of links.

Good quality link development work focuses on quality rather than quantity. A well-researched and relevant, good quality link is worth many times more than hundreds of free directory submissions. The fundamentals of link building are, have always been and always will be, based on good quality (i.e., useful, interesting, entertaining, educational) content. Because if there is no good content on your site that people can link to, it will be very difficult to convince them to do so.

Code Optimization

Code optimization is a service you can expect at the highest levels of SEO services, as it involves an overhaul of your website HTML. The optimization of your HTML can impact search engine rankings in two ways. First, it can help alleviate code-clutter, and present your content in an easy-to-understand (for machines, that is, search engine algorithms) format. Second, it can help reduce the load-time of your website pages, so that search engine spiders don't have to wait around while your page loads (because it's too long, or has too many images, etc). A comprehensive SEO campaign will have all the above elements, but it will also incorporate other important services such as keyword research, ranking reports, traffic reports, and conversion tracking.

SEO is important whether you're a seasoned ecommerce veteran or just starting to sell online.

Optimizing your site will be a continuous process, as search engines are constantly surveying the internet to index and rank pages.

CHAPTER 5

5 SEO Hacks You Can Do Right Now to Rank Your Website Higher

Content Promotion

A website's real attraction is its content; thus, it really doesn't make sense to optimize your content and then stop dead with the optimization as soon as you hit "publish." Optimized promotion includes these basic strategies:

- **Post Keywords:** Use your target keyword phrase as well as one or two secondary yet related phrases in your posts sharing social content. This is particularly important on platforms that go into search results: LinkedIn, Google+, and Facebook.

- **Use Hashtags**: Preferably based on your keyword phrases.

- **Answer Queries with Content:** Respond

to queries on Yahoo Answers, Quora, and Reddit with your relevant links to content.

- **Use Voting & Social Bookmarking Sites:** Search voting sites and social bookmarking sites for keyword optimized categories you can post it. These categories tend to feature submissions with the most votes, so if you've got great content, submit it for votes.

- **Link with Similar Content:** Find other pieces of content that mention your keyword phrases and ask their owners to link up with your related content.

- **Recycle & Repurpose Great Content:** Today's blog post can be tomorrow's podcast, and so on. Repurpose in smart ways and remember to link new and older pieces of content.

Analyze Traffic Drops Using Tools

Every site experiences drops in traffic. Your task is to watch yours, determine what caused them, and fix problems as they happen. Here's how to assess a decrease in traffic:

First, check your running list of changes to the website. Larger companies should save this running list in Google Docs and use Google Analytics to annotate it. You're checking the list to see if someone on your team made changes to the site that could hurt your SEO. Next check your analytics to see that it is properly installed, currently working and hasn't been jeopardized. You are making sure that what you're seeing is a drop in organic search traffic rather than an error in analytics tracking. Once you confirm that it isn't a tracking error, compare the time periods just after and just before the drop for your landing pages, top keywords, top browsers, top search engines, top devices, top regions, and top languages to see where you lost traffic. Make a note of this and continue.

Now, check your webmaster tools. Find out if your site has been hit by Google with a penalty by looking for alert messages in Google Search Console. If you've been penalized by Google, fix whatever problem caused the penalty and re-submit your site. You're also looking for crawling errors, duplicate content, sitemap errors, manual actions, and essential images or URLs that are blocked by "robots.txt", to name a few examples. Now, check your ranking tools like Moz, SEM Rush, Search Metrics and even GA. When you check these tools look at the visibility index for your top keywords, changes in your keywords per page, losses and gains in ranking, and local rankings. This should give you more insight into what happened to your traffic. Next use a third party tool to conduct a link analysis. This should help you identify Penguin penalties and negative SEO. Some signs of negative SEO include: fake social media profiles trolling you, loss of backlinks, and spammed anchor texts.

Remember, when your site experiences a drop in SEO traffic, check your analytics first, your webmaster tools second, your website third and backlink profile fourth. If you don't have the answer at that point, check for Google updates on larger websites like SeroundTable and SearchEngineland.

Improve Your Content

For some keywords to achieve the best search results with the best content relative to the keyword, Google and other Search Engines are constantly on the lookout for the quality of content web-pages that provide the relative content. Hence it is imperative that your webpage should have the best content available. There are some specific kinds of content that these Search Engines highlight:

- **Automatically generated content:** Using

content spinning, translator, and other machine-generated content programs gives you thin, auto-generated content that Google hates.

- **Boilerplate Content:** This happens most on sites that are all offering the same products for sale. Remember, even a product description benefits from adding your brand voice and insight to the mix.

- **Scraped Content:** This is content that is just republished or modified only a little. Remember to add value and your own commentary to anything that you found elsewhere.

- **Doorway Pages:** These pages are created to manipulate web crawlers to produce a better rank for some queries. If the sole purpose of a page is to take searchers somewhere else, it may be a doorway page.

Refrain from Large Images

Often, designers or content creators don't consider the file size or resolution of an image before adding it to a page. They won't reduce an image to the maximum size needed on the page, nor will they save it at an appropriate resolution. A 600-dpi image that was "resized" to be tiny using the width and height attributes in an IMG tag isn't merely lazy; it's an affront to website visitors. A huge image (as large as 6 MB) can substantially slow down the time it takes for the page to load, hurting both your rankings and the user experience (and consequently, the site's conversion rate). It is incredibly easy to optimize that image to a more reasonable size and then re-upload it. This is probably the number one "quick hack" for improving your site speed. Use a tool like WebPageTest to check the file sizes of all the elements on a page. (Or you can use the Developer Tools built into the Chrome browser) Check your images, and have your designers optimize them. Train the people who create and upload your content to get into the habit of checking image sizes before they publish anything.

Improve Web Page Performance

Well performing websites enjoy higher visitor engagement, retention and conversion. Given how fickle users can be, plus the fact that mobile devices are very significant these days, never has the speed of websites been so important. You can help your site run faster as a matter of course if you make speed an ongoing priority:

- **Old Plug-ins:** Search for unused plug-ins and themes and get rid of them. Don't just deactivate them, because outdated plug-ins can be a security risk.

- **Enable Gzip Compression:** This lets your server use smaller file sizes which in turn means they load faster. Gzip compression can spare your server the work of loading around fifty to seventy percent of original file sizes.

- **Above-the-fold first:** Focus on optimizing your above-the-fold region first to boost speed right when a visitor comes to your page.

- **Minimize Redirects:** Try to use redirects only as needed; streamline your structure regularly to minimize redirects.

- **Minify Resources:** Minifying resources just means compressing your CSS, HTML, and JavaScript code. There are services and tools for this if you don't know how to do it. You can also work with a developer, or if you're using WordPress, research how to minify within the WordPress theme you're using.

Conclusion

Thank you again for downloading this book!

I hope this book could help you to give you an overall understanding of the concept, usability and the operations of SEO in marketing, which in hand can be a useful tool for the success of your business.

The next step is to take in and fully understand these concepts and strategies by reading it thoroughly several times. Consider which strategy is suitable to your requirements and your website so that it may thrive and standout, leading to guaranteed marketing success.

Finally, if you enjoyed this book, then I'd like to ask you for a favor, would you be kind enough to leave a review for this book on Amazon? It'd be greatly appreciated!

Click here to leave a review for this book on Amazon!

Thank you and good luck!

Preview Of Snapchat Marketing For Business

Social Media Marketing Strategies

There are two basic strategies for engaging on social media:

Passive Approach

Social media can be a useful source of market information and a way to hear customer perspectives. Blogs, content communities, and forums are platforms where individuals share their reviews and recommendations of brands, products, and services. Businesses are able to tap and analyze the customer voices and feedback generated in social media for marketing purposes; in this sense the social media is a relatively inexpensive source of market intelligence which can be used by marketers and managers to track and respond to consumer-identified problems and detect market opportunities. For example, the Internet erupted with videos and pictures of iPhone 6 "bend test" which showed that the coveted phone could be bent by hand pressure. The so-called "bend gate" controversy created confusion amongst customers who had waited months for the launch of the latest rendition of the iPhone. However, Apple promptly issued a statement saying that the problem was extremely rare and that the company had taken several steps to make the mobile device's case stronger and robust. Unlike traditional market research methods such as surveys, focus groups, and data mining which are time-consuming and costly, and which take weeks or even months to analyze, marketers can use social media to obtain 'live' or "real time" information about consumer behavior and viewpoints on a company's brand or products. This can be useful in the highly dynamic, competitive fast-paced and global marketplace of the 2010s.

Active Approach

Social media can be used not only as public relations and direct marketing tools but also as communication channels targeting very specific audiences with social media influencers and social media personalities and as effective customer engagement tools. Technologies predating social media, such as broadcast TV and newspapers can also provide advertisers with a targeted audience, given that an ad placed during a sports game broadcast or in the sports section of a newspaper is likely to be read by sports fans. However, social media websites can target niche markets even more precisely. Using digital tools such as Google Ad-Sense, advertisers can target their ads to very specific demographics, such as people who are interested in social entrepreneurship, political activism associated with a particular political party, or video gaming. Google Ad-Sense does this by looking for keywords in social media user's online posts and comments. It would be hard for a TV station or paper-based newspaper to provide ads that are this targeted (though not impossible, as can be seen with "special issue" sections on niche issues, which newspapers can use to sell targeted ads).

However, there are certain strategic steps that a company may adapt in order to enhance its social perception and promotion through social media marketing.

1. Identify Business Goals

Every piece of your social media strategy serves the goals you set. You simply can't move forward without knowing what you're working toward.

Look closely at your company's overall needs and decide how you want to use social media to contribute to reaching them.

You'll undoubtedly come up with several personalized goals, but there are a few that all companies should include in their strategy—increasing brand awareness, retaining customers and reducing marketing costs are relevant to everyone. I suggest you choose two primary goals and two secondary goals to focus on. Having too many goals distracts you and you'll end up achieving none.

2. Set Marketing Objectives

Goals aren't terribly useful if you don't have specific parameters that define when each is achieved. For example, if one of your primary goals is generating leads and sales, how many leads and sales do you have to generate before you consider that goal a success?

Marketing objectives define how you get from Point A (an unfulfilled goal) to Point B (a successfully fulfilled goal). You can determine your objectives with the S-M-A-R-T approach: Make your objectives specific, measurable, achievable, relevant and time-bound.

Using our previous example, if your goal is to generate leads and sales, a specific marketing objective may be to increase leads by 50%. In order to measure your progress, choose which analytics and tracking tools you need to have in place. Setting yourself up for failure is never a good idea. If you set an objective of increasing sales by 1,000%, it's doubtful you'll meet it. Choose objectives you can achieve, given the resources you have. You've taken the time to refine your goals so they're relevant to your company, so extend that same consideration to your objectives. If you want to get support from your C-level executives, ensure your objectives are relevant to the company's overall vision.

Attaching a timeframe to your efforts is imperative. When do you intend to achieve your goal(s)? Next month? By the end of this year?

Your objective of increasing leads by 50% may be specific, measurable, achievable and relevant, but if you don't set a deadline for achieving the goal, your efforts, resources and attention may be pulled in other directions.

3. Identify Ideal Customers

If a business is suffering from low engagement on their social profiles, it's usually because they don't have an accurate ideal customer profile. Buyer personas help you define and target the right people, in the right places, at the right times with the right messages.

When you know your target audience's age, occupation, income, interests, pains, problems, obstacles, habits, likes, dislikes, motivations and objections, then it's easier and cheaper to target them on social or any other media. The more specific you are, the more conversions you're going to get out of every channel you use to promote your business.

4. Research Competition

When it comes to social media marketing, researching your competition not only keeps you apprised of their activity, it gives you an idea of what's working so you can integrate those successful tactics into your own efforts. Start by compiling a list of at least 3-5 main competitors. Search which social networks they're using and analyze their content strategy. Look at their number of fans or followers, posting frequency and time of day. Also pay attention to the type of content they're posting and its context (humorous, promotional, etc.) and how they're responding to their fans.

The most important activity to look at is engagement. Even though page admins are the only ones who can calculate engagement rate on a particular update, you can get a good idea of what they're seeing.

For example, let's say you're looking at a competitor's last 20-30 Facebook updates. Take the total number of engagement activities for those posts and divide it by the page's total number of fans. (Engagement activity includes likes, comments, shares, etc.)

You can use that formula on all of your competitors' social profiles (e.g., on Twitter you can calculate retweets and favorites). Keep in mind that the calculation is meant to give you a general picture of how the competition is doing so you can compare how you stack up against each other.

5. Choose Channels and Tactics

Many businesses create accounts on every popular social network without researching which platform will bring the most return. You can avoid wasting your time in the wrong place by using the information from your buyer personas to determine which platform is best for you. If your prospects or customers tell you they spend 40% of their online time on Facebook and 20% on Twitter, you know which primary and secondary social networks you should focus on.

When your customers are using a specific network, that's where you need to be—not everywhere else. Your tactics for each social channel rely on your goals and objectives, as well as the best practices of each platform. For example, if your goal is increasing leads and your primary social network is Facebook, some effective tactics are investing in Facebook advertising or promotion campaigns to draw more attention to your lead magnets.

6. Create a Content Strategy

Content and social media have a symbiotic relationship: Without great content social media is meaningless and without social media nobody will know about your content. Use them together to reach and convert your prospects.

There are three main components to any successful

social media content strategy: type of content, time of posting and frequency of posting.

The type of content you should post on each social network relies on form and context. Form is how you present that information—text only, images, links, video, etc.

Context fits with your company voice and platform trends. Should your content be funny, serious, highly detailed and educational or something else?

There are many studies that give you a specific time when you should post on social media. However, I suggest using those studies as guidelines rather than hard rules. Remember, your audience is unique, so you need to test and figure out the best time for yourself.

Posting frequency is as important as the content you share. You don't want to annoy your fans or followers, do you?

Finding the perfect frequency is crucial because it could mean more engagement for your content or more unlikes and unfollows. Use Facebook Insights to see when your fans are online and engaging with your content.

7. Allocate Budget and Resources

To budget for social media marketing, look at the tactics you've chosen to achieve your business goals and objectives. Make a comprehensive list of the tools you need (e.g., social media monitoring, email marketing and CRM), services you'll outsource (e.g., graphic design or video production) and any advertising you'll purchase. Next to each, include the annual projected cost so you can have a high-level view of what you're investing in and how it affects your marketing budget.

Many businesses establish their budget first, and then select which tactics fit that budget. I take the opposite approach. I establish a strategy first, and then determine the budget that fits that strategy.

If your strategy execution fees exceed your budget estimate, prioritize your tactics according to their ROI timeframe. The tactics with the fastest ROI (e.g., advertising and social referral) take priority because they generate instant profit you can later invest into long-term tactics (fan acquisition, quality content creation or long-term engagement).

8. Assign Roles

Knowing who's responsible for what increases productivity and avoids confusion and overlapping efforts. Things may be a bit messy in the beginning, but with time team members will know their roles and what daily tasks they're responsible for.

When everyone knows his or her role, it's time to start planning the execution process. You can either plan daily or weekly. I don't advise putting a monthly plan together because lots of things will come up and you may end up wasting time adapting to the new changes. You can use tools like Basecamp or ActiveCollab to manage your team and assign tasks to each member. These tools save you tons of time and help you stay organized.

Click here to check out the rest of Snapchat Marketing For Business on Amazon.

Or go to: bit.ly/SnapchatBook

More from Tony Robson:
If you enjoyed this book and are interested in reading

more of my work, feel free to click the links below, which will take you directly to the product page on Amazon. Just click on the books that interest you and it will take you right to the Amazon page. Enjoy!

Marketing / Business Ebooks
Snapchat Marketing For Business: An Entrepreneur's Guide to Snapchat Marketing Mastery For Business Success!

The Art of the Deal: An Entrepreneur's Guide to Negotiation, Money Management, and Business Success

Children's Health
Mindfulness For Children: The Natural Way to Cure ADHD, Improve Focus and Schoolwork, and Have a Happy and Healthy Child

ADHD Diet For Children: Recipes and Diet to Help Your Child Focus, Perform Better at School, and Overcome ADHD For Life

Diet and Nutrition
Ketogenic Cookbook: Keto Diet Cookbook with Simple and Delicious Breakfast, Lunch, Dinner, Dessert, and BONUS Smoothie Recipes

Bulletproof Diet Cookbook For Beginners: Quick and Easy Recipes and Smoothies to Lose Fat and Increase Energy

Adult Health and Wellness
Mindfulness For Beginners: Simple Mindfulness Guide and Mindfulness Meditation Techniques for Stress Reduction and Anxiety Relief

Tooth Decay: Natural Tooth Decay Cure with Simple Treatments to Prevent Tooth Decay For Life

Self Help
Public Speaking: Overcome Public Speaking Fear and Anxiety For Magic Success and Confidence

The Art of Peace and Aikido: An Introduction to The Art of peace and Aikido For Spiritual Awakening

Connect with Tony Robson:
Tony Robson Author Page
Tony Robson Facebook Page
Tony Robson Twitter Page

www.ingramcontent.com/pod-product-compliance
Lightning Source LLC
Chambersburg PA
CBHW050017230526
45470CB00003B/1013